D0436318

This little book
of love
belongs to

_____

May you have warm words on a cold evening, a full moon on a dark night, and the road downhill all the way to your door.

A Good Marriage

by
Mary Engelbreit

Andrews and McMeel
A Universal Press Syndicate Company
Kansas City

10 9 8 7 6 5 4

ISBN: 0-8362-4601-2

Library of Congress Catalog Card Number: 91-78257

There is no more lovely, friendly, and charming relationship, communion, or company than a good marriage.
—Anon.

A Good Marriage

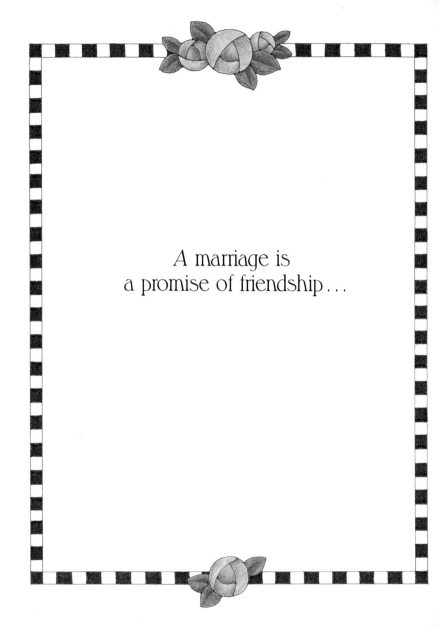

*A marriage is
a promise of friendship...*

a promise of shelter…

Flowers are lovely; love is flower-like; Friendship is a sheltering tree.

Coleridge

shared dreams…

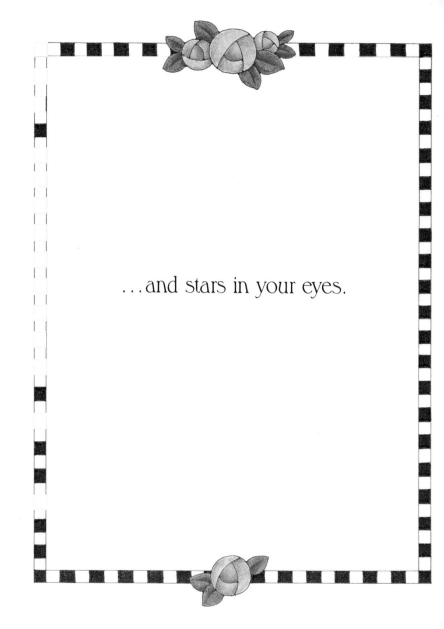

...and stars in your eyes.

GROW OL
THE BEST I

19 ME 85

*A marriage is
a promise of love…*

a promise to
offer a heart…

HERE.

...a helping hand,
and a shoulder to lean on.

LOVE COMFORTETH
LIKE SUNSHINE
AFTER RAIN
WILLIAM SHAKESPEARE

A PLACE FOR EVERY THING

···AND
EVERY·
··THING
IN····IT'S
PLACE

A marriage is
a promise to laugh...

IT TAKES A MIGHTY GOOD HUSBAND TO BE BETTER THAN NONE

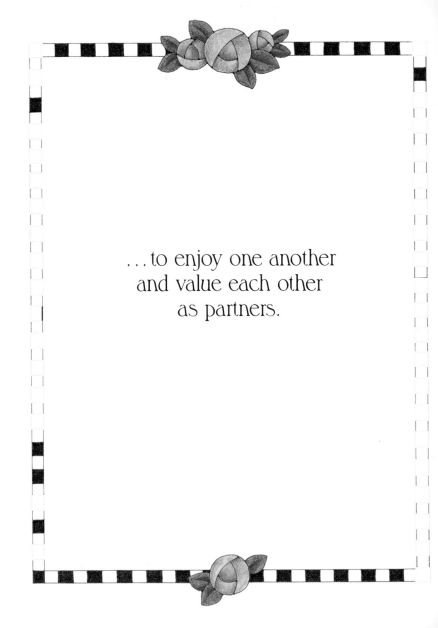

... to enjoy one another
and value each other
as partners.

I COULD HAVE DANCED ALL NIGHT.

A marriage is a promise—
the beautiful and lasting promise
to live "happily ever after."